from SEA TO SHINING SEA

Nebraska

By Dennis Brindell Fradin

CONSULTANTS

Frederick C. Luebke, Ph.D., Charles Mach Professor of History Emeritus,
University of Nebraska–Lincoln

Robert L. Hillerich, Ph.D., Professor Emeritus, Bowling Green State University;
Consultant, Pinellas County Schools, Florida

CHILDRENS PRESS®
CHICAGO

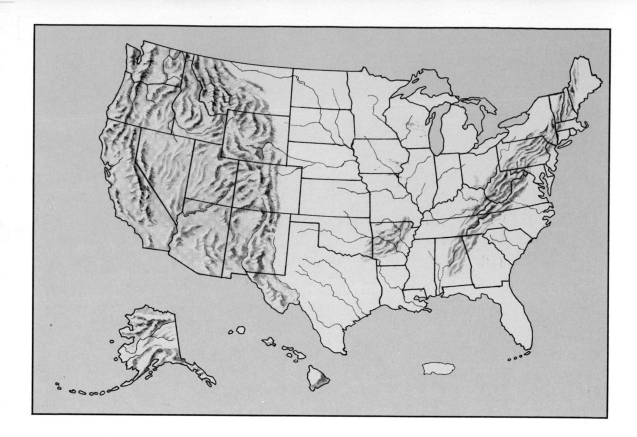

Nebraska is one of the twelve states in the region called the Midwest. The other Midwest states are Illinois, Indiana, Iowa, Kansas, Michigan, Minnesota, Missouri, North Dakota, Ohio, South Dakota, and Wisconsin.

For the reference librarians at the Skokie Public Library, Skokie, Illinois, with gratitude for their help over many years

Front cover picture: A soybean field near Falls City; page 1: Pine Ridge view toward the Black Hills, Chadron State Park; back cover: Pinnacle at Niobrara River, Fort Niobrara Wilderness

Project Editor: Joan Downing
Design Director: Karen Kohn
Research Assistant: Judith Bloom Fradin
Typesetting: Graphic Connections, Inc.
Engraving: Liberty Photoengraving

Library of Congress Cataloging-in-Publication Data

Fradin, Dennis B.
  Nebraska / by Dennis Brindell Fradin.
    p.   cm. — (From sea to shining sea)
  Includes index.
  ISBN 0-516-03827-3
  1. Nebraska—Juvenile literature. [1. Nebraska.] I. Title.
  II. Series: Fradin, Dennis B. From sea to shining sea.
F666.3.F68   1995   95-12951
978.2—dc20   CIP
                                                        AC

Table of Contents

Children carrying flags from around the world in Lincoln's Star City Holiday Parade

Introducing the Cornhusker State

Nebraska is part of the midwestern United States. The state's name comes from the Oto Indian word *nebrathka*. It means "flat water." Nebrathka was the Oto name for Nebraska's Platte River.

For many years, Nebraska belonged to the Native Americans. It was part of the "Great American Desert." American explorers said Nebraska was too dry for farming. In the 1860s, large numbers of pioneers started settling Nebraska. By the 1890s, Nebraska was a great farming state. Its farmers used irrigation to grow large corn crops. Many Nebraskans also raised cattle.

Today, Nebraska is one of the world's great farming regions. It is a top cattle, hog, and corn producer. Omaha is a good livestock market. Nebraskans also make many goods. They range from processed foods to farm machinery.

A picture map of Nebraska

The Cornhusker State is special in other ways, too. Where did Arbor Day begin? Where is Boys Town? Which is the only state with a one-house legislature? Where were Malcolm X, President Gerald Ford, and author Mari Sandoz born? The answer is: Nebraska!

Overleaf: The Badlands, Scotts Bluff National Monument

5

Plains, Sand Hills,
and River Valleys

Plains, Sand Hills, and River Valleys

Only fourteen of the other forty-nine states are larger than Nebraska.

A field with soybeans and corn near Rulo

On a map, Nebraska looks like a train's locomotive heading east. The state covers 77,355 square miles of the Midwest. Six states border Nebraska. South Dakota is to the north. Iowa and Missouri are to the east. Kansas lies to the south. Colorado is to the southwest. Wyoming is Nebraska's neighbor to the west.

Plains cover all of Nebraska. These are rather flat lands. The Dissected Till Plains are in the easternmost part of the state. Corn and soybeans grow well in the rich soil. This rolling land is cut by many streams. The Great Plains cover the rest of the state. The Sand Hills rise in the middle of the Great Plains. Over time, wind piled up sand to form these hills. Grasses hold down the sand. Cattle graze on the grasses. Northwestern Nebraska has many strange rock formations. Deep canyons cut through this land. Tall buttes rise above it.

Water, Plants, and Wildlife

The Missouri River forms Nebraska's eastern and northeastern borders. Another major river is the

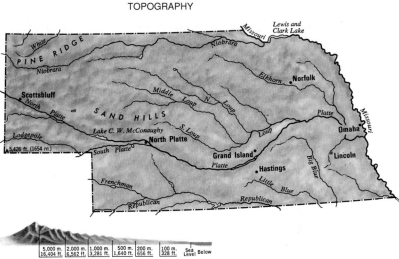

| 5,000 m. 16,404 ft. | 2,000 m. 6,562 ft. | 1,000 m. 3,281 ft. | 500 m. 1,640 ft. | 200 m. 656 ft. | 100 m. 328 ft. | Sea Level | Below |

Platte. It snakes across the middle of Nebraska. The North Platte and South Platte rivers join to form the Platte. The Niobrara flows through northern Nebraska. The Republican River runs across the south.

The Cornhusker State has about 2,000 lakes. Most are small natural lakes in the Sand Hills. Nebraska also has a number of artificially made lakes. Lake McConaughy is the largest of these lakes. It covers 55 square miles. Lake McConaughy was formed by damming the North Platte River.

Left: The Niobrara River in Cherry County

9

Red fox

About 80 percent of the world's sandhill cranes visit the Platte River area each spring. These birds have long, thin legs.

Pronghorn antelope

Nebraska is one of the least-wooded states. But there are more trees now than there were when the settlers arrived. The cottonwood is the state tree. Elms, oaks, pines, and cedars are other Nebraska trees. Many kinds of wildflowers grow in the state. Goldenrod is the state flower. Tall prairie grasses grow in eastern Nebraska. Short grasses grow in the west.

The western meadowlark is the state bird. Ducks, geese, and wild turkeys are other Nebraska birds. Every spring, huge numbers of sandhill cranes gather in Nebraska. Deer and elk live there. So do pronghorn antelopes. They can run 60 miles per hour. Coyotes, foxes, prairie dogs, and jackrabbits are other Nebraska animals. Catfish and trout are among the state's fish.

CLIMATE

Nebraska has hot summers and cold winters. Summer temperatures often reach above 90 degrees Fahrenheit in parts of the state. In winter, temperatures sometimes fall below 0 degrees Fahrenheit. Rainfall across Nebraska ranges from 18 to 34 inches. Western Nebraska receives less rain than eastern Nebraska. The same is true of snowfall. About 30

inches of snow falls in the east each year. Less falls in the west. Periods of little rain and snow cause droughts. These dry spells can kill crops.

Nebraska has many storms throughout the year. Rainstorms sometimes cause floods. Each winter, parts of Nebraska suffer blizzards. These snowstorms are driven by strong winds. About seventy tornadoes a year strike Nebraska. These whirling windstorms destroy crops and buildings. They can also kill people. Nebraska is also subject to hail. These balls of ice also cause damage.

Courthouse Rock and Jail Rock, western Nebraska

Overleaf: Fort Kearney State Historical Park

11

From Ancient Times Until Today

FROM ANCIENT TIMES UNTIL TODAY

Long ago, many animals that no longer exist roamed Nebraska. A rhinoceros as small as a pony lived there. Pigs 7 feet tall made their homes in Nebraska. Beavers the size of men lived there, too. Giant sloths, an ancient species of bison, and even camels also lived in Nebraska. Mastodons and mammoths roamed about. The world's largest mammoth skeleton was found near North Platte. This elephant-like animal was nearly 13.5 feet tall. That's taller than the largest modern elephant.

About 2 million years ago, the Ice Age began. During that time, glaciers covered eastern Nebraska. These slowly moving sheets of ice helped form the state's rich soil.

A petroglyph (an ancient rock carving) at Indian Cave State Park

AMERICAN INDIANS

The first people reached Nebraska about 12,000 years ago. This was at the end of the Ice Age. These early Nebraskans hunted mammoths and giant bison with spears. Later, some of these people farmed and made pottery.

Much later, many American Indian groups moved into Nebraska. The Pawnee were Nebraska's largest group. They built villages in eastern and southern Nebraska. Their homes were called earth lodges. They were made of wood, grass, and mud. The Pawnee hunted buffalo. But they were mainly farmers. The Pawnee planted corn, squash, and beans. The Oto, Missouri, Omaha, and Ponca also farmed Nebraska's rich land.

Other Indians in Nebraska were mainly hunters. They were the Sioux, Cheyenne, Comanche, and

Pawnee chiefs and warriors

Arapaho. These Indians followed the buffalo herds. They lived in tepees. These cone-shaped tents were made of animal skins. They were easy to move.

EUROPEAN AND AMERICAN EXPLORERS AND FUR TRADERS

By the 1700s, both Spain and France claimed land in North America. Nebraska was included in their claims. Étienne Veniard de Bourgmont was one of the first Europeans known to enter Nebraska. This Frenchman explored the Missouri River to the mouth of the Platte River in 1714. Spanish soldiers tried to push the French out of Nebraska in 1720. The Pawnee attacked and defeated the Spaniards. French brothers Paul and Pierre Mallet reached Nebraska in 1739.

French fur traders also came. They traded with the Indians. The French exchanged kettles and beads for beaver furs and deerskins.

By 1732, England had thirteen colonies along the Atlantic Ocean. These colonies declared their independence in 1776. That was the beginning of the United States.

In 1803, the United States bought France's North American lands. Nebraska was part of this land purchase. In 1804, Meriwether Lewis and William Clark began exploring the new land. They traveled up the Missouri River. In August, they met with Indians near present-day Omaha.

In the early 1800s, more fur traders came to Nebraska. Fur-trader Manuel Lisa built outposts in Nebraska. A major post was Fort Lisa. It was begun in 1812, near present-day Omaha. Army posts were also built. They protected fur traders and travelers in Nebraska. In 1819, the army started building Fort Atkinson. It was also near present-day Omaha.

THE NEBRASKA TERRITORY AND STATEHOOD

People began to travel by wagon across Nebraska to Oregon in the early 1840s. They followed the Oregon Trail from the Missouri River up the Platte and North Platte rivers. Thousands of pioneers traveled west through Nebraska. They weren't supposed to settle in Nebraska. It was still Indian land. But some broke the law by settling there. In 1854, the United States government passed the Kansas-Nebraska Act. Kansas and Nebraska became territories. They were opened to settlement.

Eastern Nebraska was settled first. Towns sprang up along and near the Missouri River. Bellevue,

The Bordeaux Trading Post at the Museum of the Fur Trade in Chadron

Omaha, Nebraska City, Grand Island, and Beatrice were begun by 1857. The Homestead Act of 1862 boosted settlement. For a small fee, people received 160 acres of land. They had to live on and work the land for five years. Then the land was theirs. Daniel Freeman claimed to be the first homesteader under this act. He and his wife Agnes built a log cabin. They lived near Beatrice.

Many homesteads lacked trees for lumber. In such places, Nebraskans cut grassy chunks of the earth into bricks. With the bricks, they built sod houses. The pioneers called the sod "Nebraska mar-

Left: The C. H. LaForge sod house in Custer County
Right: The Cal Snyder ranch at Milburn

ble." Flowers grew on their rooftops. But snakes and worms sometimes dropped into the homes. With little wood around, the pioneers often burned cow manure. They called it "Nebraska coal."

On March 1, 1867, Nebraska became the thirty-seventh state. David Butler was its first state governor. David City and Butler County were named for him. Lincoln became the permanent capital.

On April 10, 1872, the new state held the first Arbor Day. This was Julius Sterling Morton's idea. He lived in Nebraska City. Morton had planted many trees on his land. He wanted all Nebraskans to plant trees. This would improve the soil. Trees' roots hold water in the ground. About 1 million trees were planted on Nebraska's first Arbor Day. Now, Nebraska's Arbor Day is held on April 22. That was Morton's birthday. Many other states also set aside an Arbor Day for tree-planting.

RANCHERS, INDIAN FIGHTS, AND FARM PROBLEMS

J. Sterling Morton

Thousands of settlers moved into western Nebraska in the late 1800s. Many began cattle ranches. Towns sprang up in western Nebraska. However, they never grew as large as eastern Nebraska's cities.

Sioux leader Crazy Horse was murdered at the guardhouse, Fort Robinson (above).

Meanwhile, the Indians were being pushed off Nebraska's land. At times, they fought back. In 1864, the Sioux and other western tribes attacked wagon trains, stagecoaches, and ranches. But they were finally defeated. In 1877, Sioux leader Crazy Horse surrendered at Fort Robinson. Then a soldier at the fort murdered him. By 1879, fighting between Indians and whites ended. Most of Nebraska's Indians were sent to reservations in Nebraska, South Dakota, and Oklahoma.

Nebraska's farmers suffered rough times in the late 1800s. Grasshoppers destroyed their crops (1874-1877). Blizzards killed people and livestock in the 1880s. The Schoolchildren's Blizzard of January 1888 struck during a school day. Many children couldn't find their way home. More than 200 people died. In 1890-1894, drought dried up crops.

Western Nebraska never had enough water for most kinds of farming. Irrigation was needed in such places. In 1895, the state set up the Board of Irrigation. In 1902, the United States government passed the Reclamation Act. It provided federal money for irrigation. Since then, Nebraska has built many irrigation projects. Today, about 11,000 square miles of Nebraska are irrigated.

Some of Nebraska's farm problems were man-made. Railroads' prices for shipping crops and farm

Irrigation means bringing water to farms by man-made methods such as damming rivers or digging ditches.

An early irrigation canal being built at the Platte River

William Jennings Bryan

goods were high. Yet, prices paid to farmers were low. Farmers also had trouble receiving bank loans.

In 1892, the Populist Party was formed. It tried to help farmers and other workers. This new party had strong support in Nebraska. Many Populists were elected as state lawmakers in the 1890s. William Jennings Bryan was a Nebraska Democrat. He had moved there from Illinois. Bryan represented Nebraska in the United States House of Representatives (1891-1895). In 1896, he ran for president. Populists across the country backed him. But he lost. The Populist Party died out in the early 1900s.

WORLD WARS AND THE GREAT DEPRESSION

In 1917, the United States entered World War I (1914-1918). Nearly 48,000 Nebraskans helped win the war. Record Nebraska crops helped feed the soldiers. Nebraska's farmers received high prices for their crops. Their land went up in value, too.

After the war, crop prices and land values fell. Many Nebraskans lost their land. This happened across the country, too. Then, the Great Depression hit the United States (1929-1939). Thousands more Nebraskans lost their farms. Factory workers lost their jobs. Many of these people left the state. Nebraska lost about 60,000 people during the 1930s. Widespread drought added to the hard times. Nebraska suffered from dust storms known as "black blizzards." They blocked out the sunlight for a time in some places.

In 1934, Nebraskans voted to have a one-house legislature. This is called a unicameral system. They did this to speed up government and to cut its costs. Nebraska is the only state with this kind of legislature. The lawmakers are called senators.

Better weather helped end the depression. So did World War II (1939-1945). Factory jobs opened up again. Workers were needed to prepare for the biggest war in history. The United States entered the war in 1941. Nebraska supplied 140,000 men and women. Huge amounts of food from Nebraska also helped win the war. Nebraska had large rainfalls in the 1940s. Farmers once again grew record crops.

RECENT CHANGES, PROBLEMS, AND SUCCESSES

After the war, Nebraska's farms grew in size. But the number of farms fell. Thousands of farm people then went to work in city factories. Nebraska's manufacturing grew. The first frozen dinner was packaged in Omaha in 1953. It became known as the TV dinner. Other kinds of food packaging also grew in importance.

In 1960, more Nebraskans lived in cities than in rural areas. In the 1980s, farmers once again had a hard time earning a living. Many Nebraskans sold their farms. Businesses that supplied farmers closed. Dozens of tiny Nebraska towns died. Thousands more Nebraskans moved from their farms to the cities.

Clean water is another important matter facing Nebraskans. In some places, farm chemicals have leaked into Nebraska's groundwater. Farm families in those communities drink bottled water. State and local agencies now check the groundwater.

The Platte River also faces threats. More than half of its water is drained off to irrigate crops or to generate electricity. Years ago, the Platte was often a mile wide in spring and early summer. Today it is much smaller. During some dry periods it nearly disappears. Many birds and fish are threatened. About 500,000 sandhill cranes stop along the Platte as they migrate northward each spring. All need water. Many Nebraskans are working to protect the Platte and its wildlife.

Nebraskans have also enjoyed much good fortune. In the 1960s, the center-pivot irrigation system came into use. These above-ground water pipes have sprinklers that water crops in huge circles. Wheels move the pipes across farm fields. These sprinklers helped Nebraska's corn crop nearly double between 1972 and 1982. In 1994, the state raised its record crop of corn used as grain. That same year, Nebraska grew a record soybean crop.

Also in 1994, Nebraska's two biggest cities had low jobless rates. Only 2 of every 100 workers were jobless in both Omaha and Lincoln. These were among the lowest jobless rates for United States cities. Steady growth should keep Nebraska strong past the year 2000.

Sandhill cranes at the Platte River near Kearney

Overleaf: The superintendent of Ashfall Fossil Beds State Historical Park brushes away dirt from the remains of a barrel-chested rhino that died about 10 million years ago.

Nebraskans and Their Work

NEBRASKANS AND THEIR WORK

Nebraska has about 1.6 million people. Only fourteen states have fewer people. More than nine out of ten Nebraskans are white. Most of their backgrounds are German, Irish, English, and Swedish.

About 60,000 black Americans live in Nebraska. About 37,000 Nebraskans are Hispanic-Americans. Most of their families came from Mexico. About 12,000 Nebraskans are American Indians. The Santee Sioux, Omaha, and Winnebago are the largest groups. Many of Nebraska's 12,000 Asian-Americans came from Vietnam.

NEBRASKANS AT WORK

As of 1994, Nebraska had the country's lowest jobless rate. Only one Nebraska worker in fifty didn't have a job. Sales and service employ half of Nebraska's 800,000 workers. About 200,000 Nebraskans sell goods. These range from seeds to sports equipment. Omaha is a telemarketing center. Many workers sell goods over the phone. About 200,000 other Nebraskans provide services. Many

A group of Nebraska children mug for the camera.

Hispanic people are of Spanish-speaking background.

Omaha Indians at a powwow

Examining feed pellets at the Ralston Purina Company in Lincoln

The Ogallala livestock auction

are doctors, nurses, or lawyers. Repairers of farm machinery and cars are also counted. Banking, insurance, and real estate employ about 50,000 other service workers. Mutual of Omaha is the country's largest private health-insurance company.

Government work employs 150,000 Nebraskans. Some of them work on military bases or Indian reservations. Others work in public schools. Education is important to Nebraskans. The state has one teacher for every fourteen students. Teachers in most other states have more students.

More than 100,000 Nebraskans manufacture goods. Foods are the top product. The state is one of the country's top-ten meat packers. Iowa Beef Processors, Inc., has the world's largest beef-processing plant. It's in Dakota City. Bread, breakfast cereal, and livestock feed are other Nebraska foods. Farm machinery is the second-largest manufactured product. Telephone equipment and other electrical goods are also made in Nebraska.

Nebraska has 55,000 farms. Farmland and ranches take up over nine-tenths of the state. About 6 million beef cattle are on its feedlots, farms, and ranches. Nebraska and Kansas are tied for second place at raising beef cattle. Only Texas raises more. Nebraska also has 5 million hogs and pigs. The

28

Harvesting wheat

Cornhusker State raises the country's third-largest corn crop. Only Iowa and Illinois grow more. Only Indiana grows more popcorn.

About 1,600 Nebraskans work at mining. Oil is the state's major mining product. Nebraska clay is used in tiles and bricks. Limestone and sandstone and gravel are other mining products.

Overleaf: The Omaha skyline behind the Central Park Mall Lagoon

A Cornhusker State Tour

A Cornhusker State Tour

Nebraska has a few large cities and many small towns. Visitors learn about Nebraska's past at its forts and pioneer homes. Boys Town and the United States Strategic Command (STRATCOM) are newer places of interest in Nebraska. Some visitors try to spot Nebraska wildlife. Others watch scientists dig for fossils.

Omaha

The Omaha skyline from Heart of America Park

Omaha is Nebraska's largest city. It's a good place to start a state tour. Omaha lies on the Missouri River. It's at the middle of Nebraska's eastern border. Founded in 1854, the city was named for the Omaha Indians. More than 335,000 people live there today.

Omaha's Joslyn Art Museum displays paintings and sculptures from around the world. The Joslyn is famous for its Karl Bodmer watercolors. Bodmer traveled up the Missouri River in the 1830s. His paintings show early Nebraska and nearby places. In 1995, a new addition to the Joslyn, designed by architect Sir Norman Foster, was added. The

addition nearly doubled the size of the museum. The Omaha Children's Museum lets visitors walk through the "Model of Omaha." This is a scaled-down model of part of the city.

Omaha's Henry Doorly Zoo has more than 2,500 animals. Its big cats include white tigers and snow leopards. Penguins, sharks, and colorful fish can be seen at the zoo's aquarium. This zoo has the world's largest indoor rain forest. Monkeys and pygmy hippos live there.

Outside Omaha is Father Edward Flanagan's Boys Town. It started in an Omaha house in 1917. Father Flanagan took in homeless and troubled

This picture of the Joslyn Art Museum was taken before the new addition was built.

boys. Since 1979, Boys Town has been home to many girls, too. Over the years, more than 18,000 young people have lived there. Visitors can tour the grounds and the Father Flanagan Museum.

OTHER EASTERN NEBRASKA HIGHLIGHTS

Besides Omaha, eight of Nebraska's ten largest cities are in the east. They are Lincoln, Grand Island, Bellevue, Kearney, Fremont, Hastings, Norfolk, and Columbus. Northwest of Omaha is Fremont. It is home to the Louis E. May Historical Museum. The museum is in a twenty-five-room mansion built in 1874. The many rooms show how homes of the 1800s looked.

Bellevue is south of Omaha. It was begun in 1823 as a fur-trading post. Bellevue is Nebraska's oldest town. Nebraska's first bank (1855) and first church (1856) are there. They have been restored. Offutt Air Force Base is outside Bellevue. The base is home to the United States Strategic Command (STRATCOM). The country's long-range missiles and bombers are controlled from there. Also at Offutt is the Strategic Air Command Museum.

Nebraska City is south of Bellevue. Arbor Lodge is there. This mansion was Julius Sterling

Offutt Air Force Base holds an annual open house.

Morton's home. On the grounds are 260 kinds of trees and shrubs. Morton planted some of them. The Allen B. Mayhew Cabin is also at Nebraska City. It was a stop on the Underground Railroad. Runaway slaves from southern states hid in the cabin's underground passage. When it was safe, the slaves crossed into Iowa. Then they headed for freedom in Canada.

Lincoln is northwest of Nebraska City. It was laid out in 1864. Today, Lincoln has about 200,000 people. It's Nebraska's second-largest city. Lincoln is also Nebraska's capital. The capitol there is one

Left: A view of Lincoln
Right: The capitol

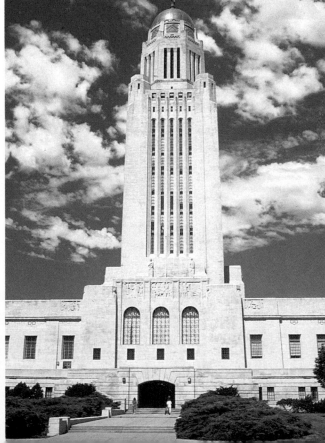

The flag line for the University of Nebraska marching band was part of Lincoln's Star City Holiday Parade.

of the most beautiful in the United States. It has a 400-foot-high tower from which visitors can view the city. On the capitol grounds is a Daniel Chester French statue of Abraham Lincoln, for whom the city was named.

The University of Nebraska is also in Lincoln. Its "Elephant Hall" in the Nebraska State Museum has mammoth bones and other fossils. The University's Sheldon Art Gallery has a major collection of American painting and sculpture. The school is also known for its football team. The

Cornhuskers were national champions in 1970, 1971, and 1994.

The Museum of Nebraska History is in Lincoln. It shows life in Nebraska from 12,000 years ago to the 1950s. Children enjoy the museum's Pawnee earth lodge of the 1860s. They also like to walk through the 1890s general store. The National Museum of Roller Skating is another Lincoln attraction. The museum displays roller skates going back to 1819.

Beatrice is south of Lincoln. It was named for eighteen-year-old Beatrice Kinney. Her father helped found the town. Pioneer homesteader Daniel Freeman lived near Beatrice. Today, his land is the Homestead National Monument. An 1872 school-house is on the grounds. There, visitors learn how important education was in Nebraska's early years.

Hastings, Kearney, and Grand Island are in the middle of southeastern Nebraska. The three towns form a triangle. The Hastings Museum has a sod house. It also shows pioneer clothing and tools.

Kearney is home to the Museum of Nebraska Art. It features works by and about Nebraskans. They include paintings by Nebraska-born artist Robert Henri. Outside Kearney, part of Fort Kearney has been restored. The fort was established in 1848.

The Palmer-Epard cabin at Homestead National Monument was built in 1867.

Today, visitors can see the fort's sod blacksmith shop.

Grand Island, founded in 1857, was moved to its present spot in 1866. Townspeople wanted to be close to the Union Pacific Railroad. The railroad was completed across Nebraska in 1867. Today, Grand Island has about 40,000 people. It's Nebraska's third-biggest city. The Stuhr Museum of the Prairie Pioneer is there. The museum's Railroad Town has sixty buildings. They show what an 1860s Nebraska railroad

Two views of the Stuhr Museum in Grand Island

town was like. Pioneer children's toys are among the museum's treasures.

Ashfall Fossil Beds State Historical Park is north of Grand Island. It's near Royal in northeast Nebraska. About 10 million years ago, a watering hole was there. About that time, a volcano erupted in Idaho. That's about 1,000 miles away. Volcanic ash drifted across northern Nebraska. Animals at the watering hole were killed. Their bones were preserved as fossils. Nearly 300 complete skeletons have come from the Fossil Beds. They include rhinoceros and horse skeletons. An 11-foot-tall camel was one of the strangest finds. Visitors can watch as more skeletons are uncovered.

Farther north is Niobrara State Park. Its bluffs rise above the Missouri River. People hike, fish, and ride horses at the park.

Three Indian reservations are in the northeast. They are the Santee Sioux, Winnebago, and Omaha reservations. Visitors are welcome at some Indian events. The Santee Sioux Powwow is held in Santee each July. The Winnebago host a powwow each July. It's held in the town of Winnebago. The Omaha's August powwow is one of the oldest festivals in North America. These Indian gatherings feature traditional dancing, foods, and beadwork.

An archaeologist at Ashfall Fossil Beds State Historical Park

A young dancer at the Omaha powwow

WESTERN NEBRASKA

The Sand Hills are in north-central Nebraska. They are the largest sand dunes area in the United States, but they are covered with grass. Therefore, cattle ranching is the Sand Hills major business. Valentine is just north of the Sand Hills. It's home to the Sandhills Museum. The museum shows tools used by the early settlers.

East of Valentine is Fort Niobrara National Wildlife Refuge. Elk, pronghorns, buffalo, and Texas longhorn cattle roam about. Several waterfalls make this refuge beautiful. To the south is Valentine National Refuge. Its lakes and marshes make good nesting spots. Canada geese, mallard ducks, and sandhill cranes are spotted there during their migration through the state.

Gordon is west of Valentine. The Cowboy Museum there has a chuck wagon. On cattle drives, cowboys were served meals from the chuck wagon. West of Gordon is Chadron. The Museum of the Fur Trade is nearby. Visitors there learn about America's fur-trading years.

Toadstool Park is in Nebraska's northwest corner. The land there is barren, dry, and rugged. Some of the park's rocks look like huge toadstools.

Toadstool Park is in the Badlands.

Agate Fossil Beds National Monument is south of Toadstool Park. Fossils from mammoths and giant pigs have been found there.

Alliance is southeast of Agate Fossil Beds National Monument. Carhenge is there. It was built with old cars in 1987. Carhenge is modeled after England's Stonehenge. About 4,000 years ago, people moved huge stones into a circle at Stonehenge. Carhenge tickles visitors' funny bones.

Scottsbluff is southwest of Alliance. It's near Nebraska's western border. This town was named for nearby Scotts Bluff. This is an 800-foot butte. It was a landmark on the Oregon Trail. Today, it is part

Carhenge

Scotts Bluff National Monument

of Scotts Bluff National Monument. People can drive or hike to the top of the bluff. The Oregon Trail Museum is at the bluff's base. There, visitors learn about the westward movement. Nearby is Chimney Rock. It was another Oregon Trail landmark. Chimney Rock rises 500 feet above the plains.

Sidney is southeast of Chimney Rock. Legion Park is there. The park's Memorial Gardens has a giant United States map. It's made of flowers and trees. The park's War Memorial honors veterans of all American wars. A giant American flag flies atop its 141-foot flagpole. Legion Park's Centennial Forest honors couples who have been married fifty years.

Ogallala is east of Sidney. The Texas Cattle Trail ended there in the 1870s and 1880s. When the cowboys were in town, many fights broke out. Front Street re-creates Ogallala's Wild West days. Each summer evening, a shootout is staged. The Cowboy Museum is part of Front Street. An old jail and schoolroom can be seen there, too.

North Platte is east of Ogallala. Scouts Rest Ranch is near North Platte. "Buffalo Bill" Cody lived there for many years. Cody was a famous Pony Express rider, army scout, and buffalo hunter. He also put together the first rodeo. Scouts Rest Ranch

Front Street, Ogallala

welcomes visitors. The Buffalo Bill Rodeo is held in North Platte in June.

Chimney Rock

McCook is south of Buffalo Bill's ranch. It's near the Kansas border. McCook is a good place to end a Nebraska tour. The George W. Norris House is there. Norris served Nebraska in the United States House of Representatives (1903-1913) and the Senate (1913-1943). He worked hard to get Nebraska's one-house legislature. Today, Norris's cradle and his mother's spinning wheels are shown at his home.

Overleaf: President Gerald Ford

43

A Gallery
of Famous
Cornhuskers

A Gallery of Famous Cornhuskers

Nebraska has produced many famous people. They include Indian chiefs, actors, authors, and a president.

Red Cloud (1822-1909) was born in Nebraska. He became a great Sioux chief. During the 1860s, Red Cloud led many battles against whites. Red Cloud's War was an Indian victory against the United States. Red Cloud forced the government to close the Bozeman Trail. It went across Indian land in Wyoming and Montana.

Joseph LaFlesche (Iron Eye) (1820-1888) was an Omaha Indian chief. Three of his children became famous. **Susette LaFlesche** (1854-1903) was born near Bellevue. She became a great speaker. Susette toured the country speaking for Indian rights. **Francis LaFlesche** (1857-1932) was also born near Bellevue. He became an anthropologist. *Middle Five: Indian Boys at School* was one of his books. **Susan LaFlesche** (1865-1915) was born in Omaha. She was one of the first American Indian women doctors. Dr. LaFlesche treated nearly every member of the Omaha tribe. She also founded a hospital on the Omaha Reservation.

The town of Red Cloud, Nebraska, was named for Chief Red Cloud (above).

Left: George Beadle
Right: Grace Abbott

Grace Abbott (1878-1939) was born in Grand Island. She became a social worker. Abbott headed the U.S. Children's Bureau (1921-1924). She improved the lives of children and their mothers. Abbott helped write the 1935 Social Security Act. This provides income for retired workers. It also grants money to widows and orphans.

George Beadle (1903-1989) was born in Wahoo. He became a scientist. Beadle studied how genes work. Genes are passed from parents to children. They decide such things as hair color and eye color. Beadle won the 1958 Nobel Prize in physiology.

Willa Cather (1873-1947) was born in Virginia. She moved to Nebraska at the age of nine. Her family settled in Red Cloud. Cather wrote stories and novels about Nebraska pioneers. *O Pioneers!* and *My Antonia* are her best-known works. John Neihardt (1881-1973) was born in Illinois. His family settled in Wayne, Nebraska, when Neihardt was ten. He became well known for his poems and other works. *Black Elk Speaks* tells a Sioux holy man's story. Mari Sandoz (1896-1966) was born in Sheridan County. Her family had a homestead in the Sand Hills. She wrote many books about life in

Left: Willa Cather
Right: Mari Sandoz

western Nebraska. *Crazy Horse* is about the Sioux warrior. Sandoz's book *Old Jules* is about her own father.

Joyce Clyde Hall (1891-1982) was born in David City. As a boy, he sold postcards door to door. Later, Hall began Hallmark Cards. It became the world's largest greeting-card company.

Many movie stars have been Nebraskans. **Harold Lloyd** (1893-1971) was born in Burchard. He became a comedian. Lloyd played shy young

Joyce Clyde Hall left most of his $100-million fortune to charity.

Harold Lloyd dangled from a skyscraper's clock in the movie Safety Last.

men who escaped from dangerous situations. He did his own stunts. In *Safety Last,* he dangled from a skyscraper's clock. **Edmund "Hoot" Gibson** (1892-1962) was born in Tekamah. His friends called him "Hoot." Gibson liked to chase owls. He learned to ride and rope on his family's ranch. Later, he became a cowboy movie star. His 300 films include *King of the Rodeo.* **Fred Astaire** (1899-1987) was born in Omaha. By the age of seven, he was dancing in traveling shows. Astaire became the most famous dancer in movie history. *Top Hat* is one of his great movies.

Left: "Hoot" Gibson Right: Fred Astaire dancing with Rita Hayworth in the movie You Were Never Lovelier

49

Henry Fonda
Marlon Brando

Darryl F. Zanuck (1902-1979) was born in Wahoo. At age eight, he played an Indian child in a Western movie. Later, Zanuck wrote movie stories for Rin-Tin-Tin, a movie-star dog. Zanuck also produced movies. *Young Mr. Lincoln* and *The Grapes of Wrath* are two of them. **Henry Fonda** (1905-1982) starred in both of these films. Fonda was born in Grand Island. He grew up in Omaha. Fonda was great at playing quiet, honest men. He won the 1981 Academy Award for best actor. It was for his role in *On Golden Pond.* **Robert Taylor** (1911-1969) was born in Filley. He, too, became a movie star. *Johnny Eager* was one of his best films.

Two more recent stars were born in Omaha. **Marlon Brando** won two Academy Awards for best actor. They were for his roles in *On the Waterfront* and *The Godfather.* **Nick Nolte** (born 1940) is known for playing restless, lonely men. He played a football player in *North Dallas Forty.* That was a fitting role. Nolte had once wanted to play pro football. **Sandy Dennis** (1937-1992) was born in Hastings. She won the 1966 Academy Award for best supporting actress for her role in *Who's Afraid of Virginia Woolf?*

Bil Baird (1904-1987) was born in Grand Island. When Baird was seven, his father made a puppet for him. Young Baird grew up to be a puppeteer. Millions of people watched his puppets on television during the 1950s. Bubbles La Rue, the dancing puppet, was one of them. Another was Heathcliff, the talking horse.

Johnny Carson was born in Iowa in 1925. He grew up in Norfolk, Nebraska. Carson wrote for television comic Red Skelton. One night Skelton was injured. Carson went on the air for him. That started Carson's career on television. For thirty years, Carson hosted the "Tonight Show."

Paul Williams was born in Omaha in 1940. He grew to be 5-feet 2-inches tall. Williams planned to become a jockey. Instead, he became an award-winning songwriter. One of his songs is "The Rainbow Connection." It's from *The Muppet Movie.*

Several famous athletes were Nebraskans. **Max Baer** (1909-1959) was born in Omaha. He was the "Merry Madcap" of boxing. Baer clowned around in and out of the ring. He became the world heavyweight champion (1934-1935).

Two Hall of Fame baseball pitchers were Nebraskans. **Grover Cleveland Alexander** (1887-1950) was born on a farm at Elba. He won 373 big-league games. Only two pitchers won more. **Bob Gibson** was born in Omaha in 1935. He was sickly as a child and nearly died. "Gibby" grew up to be

Johnny Carson
Bob Gibson

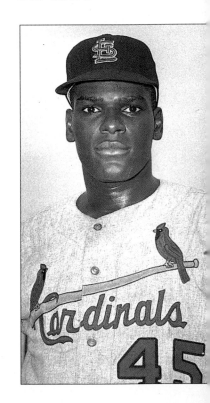

tougher than baseball spikes. He won twenty games in each of five seasons. Gibson struck out seventeen batters in a World Series game. That's an all-time World Series record.

Gerald Ford was born in Omaha in 1913. He worked his way through college washing dishes. For a time, Ford was a Yellowstone National Park ranger. Later, he served Michigan in the U.S. House of Representatives (1948-1973). In 1973-1974, he was the country's vice president. Then he served as president of the United States (1974-1977).

Malcolm X (1925-1965) was born Malcolm Little in Omaha. In his twenties, he was imprisoned for robbery. There, Malcolm X discovered the Black Muslim religion. It changed his life. After his release, Malcolm X became a great black leader. He believed that black people had the right to demand justice. Malcolm X was murdered at the age of thirty-nine. *The Autobiography of Malcolm X* helps his ideas live on.

Bob Kerrey was born in Lincoln in 1943. He lost much of his right leg in the Vietnam War. Back in Nebraska, Kerrey opened a restaurant in Omaha. About ten years later, he decided to run for governor. People said he had no chance. He won and held the office from 1983 to 1987. Since 1989, Kerrey has been a U.S. senator from Nebraska.

Bob Kerrey

Malcolm X

The birthplace of Bob Kerrey, Red Cloud, Grace Abbott, Malcolm X, and President Gerald Ford . . .

Home, too, of Willa Cather, John Neihardt, Johnny Carson, and William Jennings Bryan . . .

The only state with a one-house legislature, and the home of Boys Town . . .

Today, a giant producer of beef cattle, hogs, corn, and packaged meat . . .

This is Nebraska—the Cornhusker State!

Did You Know?

The 1938 movie *Boys Town* was about the children's home in Omaha. Spencer Tracy won the Academy Award for best actor for playing Father Edward Flanagan.

Nebraska has towns named Friend, Weeping Water, Broken Bow, Beaver City, and Wahoo.

A teenaged teacher became a heroine during the 1888 Schoolchildren's Blizzard. The wind ripped off the roof of Minnie Freeman's sod schoolhouse near Ord. Freeman tied her students to one another with string and then led them through the snow to safety. A song called "Thirteen Were Saved, or Nebraska's Fearless Maid" was composed about her.

The National Arbor Day Foundation, based in Nebraska City, has over 1 million members. Begun in 1972, the foundation is dedicated to planting trees across the country.

Omaha is home to the Ak-Sar-Ben race track, the Ak-Sar-Ben Exhibition Building, and the Ak-Sar-Ben Livestock Show and Rodeo. Ak-Sar-Ben is Nebraska spelled backward.

Song of the Great Blizzard 1888 "THIRTEEN WERE SAVED" OR NEBRASKA'S FEARLESS MAID.

SONG AND CHORUS by WM. Vincent, PUBLISHED BY LYON & HEALY, CHICAGO.

In 1898, Omaha hosted the first Log-rolling National Championship. In this sport, also called birling, two contestants stand on a log that's in a river and spin the log with their feet. Each tries to make the other fall off the log into the water.

Omaha has hosted the College World Series of baseball since 1950.

Each year for Valentine's Day, a giant heart is painted on the street in downtown Valentine. A number of couples have come to Valentine to be married on Valentine's Day.

A 1,000-mile horse race was held in June 1893. The winner, John Berry, covered the distance from Chadron, Nebraska, to Chicago, Illinois, in thirteen days, sixteen hours.

Roosevelt Park in Hebron has one of the world's largest swings. The 32-foot-long swing can hold about twenty-four children or about sixteen adults.

The Coffee Burger at Sioux Sundries in Harrison claims to make the world's largest hamburgers. They're made of two patties, for a total of 28 ounces.

Borsheim's in Omaha is the nation's largest jewelry store. Shoppers can choose from about 100,000 pieces of jewelry and other items.

The University of Nebraska Cornhuskers were once known as the Bugeaters.

NEBRASKA INFORMATION

State flag

Goldenrod

Area: 77,355 square miles (the fifteenth-biggest state)

Greatest Distance North to South: 206 miles

Greatest Distance East to West: 415 miles

Border States: South Dakota to the north; Iowa and Missouri to the east; Kansas to the south; Colorado to the southwest; Wyoming to the west

Highest Point: 5,426 feet above sea level, in Kimball County

Lowest Point: 840 feet above sea level, in Richardson County

Hottest Recorded Temperature: 118° F. (at Minden, on July 24, 1936; at Hartington, on July 17, 1936; at Geneva, on July 15, 1934)

Coldest Recorded Temperature: -47° F. (at Camp Clarke, on February 12, 1899)

Statehood: The thirty-seventh state, on March 1, 1867

Origin of Name: From the Oto Indian word *nebrathka,* which means "flat water" and was the Oto name for the Platte River

Capital: Lincoln

Counties: 93

United States Senators: 2

United States Representatives: 3

State Senators: 49

State Song: "Beautiful Nebraska," by Jim Fras (words and music) and Guy Miller (words)

State Motto: "Equality Before the Law"

Nicknames: "Cornhusker State," "Tree-planter State," "Beef State"

State Seal: Adopted in 1867

State Flag: Adopted in 1925

State Bird: Western meadowlark

State Flower: Goldenrod

State Tree: Cottonwood

State Insect: Honeybee

State Mammal: White-tailed deer

State Gemstone: Blue agate

State Rock: Prairie agate

State Fossil: Mammoth

State Grass: Little bluestem

Some Rivers: Missouri, Platte, North Platte, South Platte, Loup, North Loup, Middle Loup, South Loup, Niobrara, Elkhorn, Big Blue, Little Blue, Republican

Some Lakes: McConaughy, Merritt, Lewis and Clark, Johnson, Hugh Butler

Wildlife: Deer, elk, pronghorns, coyotes, foxes, prairie dogs, jackrabbits, bobcats, raccoons, squirrels, skunks, buffalo, western meadowlarks, ducks, geese, wild turkeys, sandhill cranes, bald eagles, pheasants, woodpeckers, crows, catfish, trout, bluegills, perch, carp, bass

Manufactured Products: Meats, breakfast cereals, bakery products, other foods, telephone equipment, other electrical goods, farm machinery, scientific and medical instruments, medicines, other chemicals

Farm Products: Beef cattle, hogs, pigs, sheep, turkeys, milk, eggs, corn, popcorn, soybeans, wheat, sorghum, oats, dry beans, sugar beets, hay, barley, potatoes, apples, honey

Mining Products: Oil, clays, sand and gravel, crushed stone, limestone

Population: 1,578,385, thirty-sixth among the states (1990 U.S. Census Bureau figures)

Major Cities (1990 Census):

Omaha	335,795	Fremont	23,680
Lincoln	191,972	Hastings	22,837
Grand Island	39,386	North Platte	22,605
Bellevue	30,982	Norfolk	21,476
Kearney	24,396	Columbus	19,480

Cottonwood tree

Western meadowlark

White-tailed deer

Nebraska History

About 10,000 B.C.—The first people reach Nebraska

1541—Spain claims a large amount of North American land, including present-day Nebraska

1682—France claims all lands drained by the Mississippi River, including Nebraska

1714—Frenchman Étienne Veniard de Bourgmont, probably the first European in Nebraska, explores the Platte River

1739—French explorers Paul and Pierre Mallet reach Nebraska

1776—The United States declares its independence from England

1803—The United States buys the land claimed by France, including Nebraska, for $15 million

1804—American explorers Meriwether Lewis and William Clark explore eastern Nebraska

1812—Fur-trader Manuel Lisa builds Fort Lisa near present-day Omaha

1819-20—The U.S. army builds Fort Atkinson near present-day Omaha

1823—Bellevue, Nebraska's oldest town, is begun as a fur-trading post

1841—The Oregon Trail opens, bringing large numbers of travelers through Nebraska

1854—The Kansas-Nebraska Act makes Kansas and Nebraska territories and opens them to settlement; Omaha is founded; Nebraska's first newspaper, the *Nebraska Palladium and Platte Valley Advocate,* is begun at Bellevue

1867—Nebraska becomes the thirty-seventh state on March 1; Lincoln becomes Nebraska's permanent capital; the Union Pacific Railroad crosses Nebraska

1871—The University of Nebraska opens

1872—J. Sterling Morton begins Arbor Day

1875—Nebraska adopts a new constitution, which is still in effect

Homesteaders making their way to new land

1877—Sioux-leader Crazy Horse surrenders at Nebraska's Fort Robinson and is murdered

1879—Fighting between Indians and whites in Nebraska ends

1888—During what is called the Schoolchildren's Blizzard, more than 200 people die

1892—The Populist Party is begun

1895—Nebraska sets up the Board of Irrigation

1896—William Jennings Bryan runs for president of the United States but loses

1902—The United States government passes the Reclamation Act, which set aside money for irrigation projects

1917—Father Edward Flanagan begins what becomes Boys Town

1917-18—Nearly 48,000 Nebraskans serve in World War I

1929-39—Farming and industry suffer nationwide during the Great Depression

1932—The State Capitol is completed in Lincoln

1934—Nebraskans vote to have a unicameral state legislature

1939—Oil is discovered in southeastern Nebraska

1941-45—Nebraska supplies 140,000 men and women plus huge amounts of food to help win World War II

1953—The first frozen TV dinner is made in Omaha

1960—For the first time, more Nebraskans live in cities than in rural areas

1967—Happy 100th birthday, Cornhusker State!

1974—Omaha-native Gerald Ford becomes the thirty-eighth president of the United States

1986—Kay Orr is the first woman elected governor of Nebraska

1990—The Cornhusker State's population is 1,578,385

1994—Nebraska grows record crops of soybeans and corn used as grain

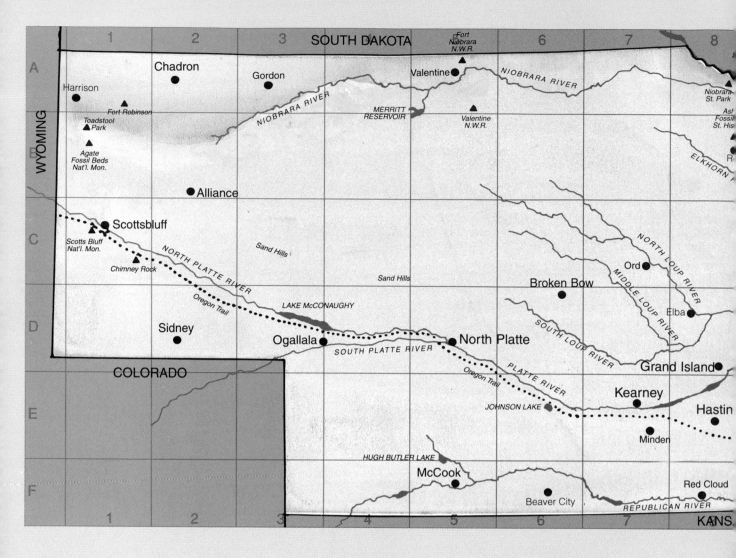

Map labels visible:

SOUTH DAKOTA

WYOMING

COLORADO

KANS.

A – Harrison, Chadron, Gordon, Valentine, Fort Niobrara N.W.R., Niobrara River, Niobrara St. Park

B – Fort Robinson, Toadstool Park, Agate Fossil Beds Nat'l. Mon., Merritt Reservoir, Valentine N.W.R., Ash Fossil St. His, Elkhorn, Alliance

C – Scottsbluff, Scotts Bluff Nat'l. Mon., Chimney Rock, North Platte River, Oregon Trail, Sand Hills, Ord, Broken Bow, Elba, North Loup River, Middle Loup River

D – Sidney, Ogallala, Lake McConaughy, South Platte River, North Platte, South Loup River, Platte River, Grand Island

E – Oregon Trail, Johnson Lake, Kearney, Hastings, Minden, Grand Island

F – Hugh Butler Lake, McCook, Beaver City, Red Cloud, Republican River

Column headers: 1 2 3 4 5 6 7 8

MAP KEY

	Burchard	F11	Geneva E9	Little Blue River F9
	Chadron	A2	Gordon A3	Loup River D8,9
	Chimney Rock	C1	Grand Island D8	McCook F5
Agate Fossil Beds	Columbus	C9	Harrison A1	Merritt Reservoir A,B4,5
National Monument B1	Dakota City	B10	Hartington A9	Middle Loup River D7
Alliance B2	David City	D10	Hastings E8	Minden E7
Ashfall Fossil Beds	Elba	D8	Hebron F9	Missouri River B11
State Historical Park B8	Elkhorn River	B8	Homestead	Nebraska City E11
Aurora E9	Filley	E11	National Monument E10	Niobrara River A,B3,4;A6
Beatrice F10	Fort Atkinson	C11	Hugh Butler Lake E5	Niobrara State Park A8
Beaver City F6	Fort Niobrara		Johnson Lake E6	Norfolk B9
Bellevue D11	National Wildlife Refuge	A5	Kearney E7	North Loup River C7,8
Big Blue River D,E10	Fort Robinson	A1	Lake McConaughy D3	North Platte D5
Boys Town D11	Fremont	C10	Lewis and Clark Lake A9	North Platte River C2
Broken Bow D6	Friend	E9	Lincoln D10	Offutt Air Force Base D11

60

GLOSSARY

blizzard: A snowstorm driven by very high winds

butte: A steep, flat-topped hill that rises sharply above the nearby land

canyon: A deep, steep-sided valley

capital: The city that is the seat of government

capitol: The building where the government meets

drought: A period when rainfall is well below normal in an area

earth lodge: An Indian home made of wood, grass, and mud

fossil: The remains of an animal or plant that lived long ago

glacier: A mass of slowly moving ice

hail: Small balls of ice that fall from the sky

homesteader: A pioneer who obtained land by paying a small fee and living on it and improving it for a number of years

irrigation: The watering of land by artificial means such as dammed water and ditches

61

manufacturing: The making of products

million: A thousand thousand (1,000,000)

plains: Rather flat lands

pollute: To harm the air, water, or land by making it dirty

population: The number of people in a place

powwow: A get-together of American Indians

rodeo: A contest in which cowboys and cowgirls ride horses and rope cattle

sod house: A home built of large, flat chunks cut from the ground and bonded by grass roots

territory: The name for a part of the United States before it became a state

tornado: A powerful windstorm that comes from a whirling, funnel-shaped cloud

wildlife refuge: A place where animals are protected

PICTURE ACKNOWLEDGMENTS

Front cover, ©**Tom Dietrich**; 1, ©**Tom Till**; 2, **Tom Dunnington**; 3, ©**Tom Tidball**; 4-5, **Tom Dunnington**; 6-7, ©M. Schneiders/**H. Armstrong Roberts**; 8, ©**Tom Dietrich**; 9 (left), ©Willard Clay/**Tony Stone Images, Inc.**; 9 (right), **Courtesy of Hammond Incorporated, Maplewood, New Jersey**; 10 (top), ©Robert Winslow/**Tom Stack & Associates**; 10 (bottom), ©Rod Planck/**Dembinsky Photo Assoc.**; 11, ©M. Schneiders/**H. Armstrong Roberts**; 12-13, ©G. Alan Nelson/**Dembinsky Photo Assoc.**; 14, ©**Tom Till**; 15, **Nebraska State Historical Society**, #I296: 2-6; 17, ©**Reinhard Brucker**; 18 (left), **The Bettmann Archive**; 18 (right), **Nebraska State Historical Society**, #D1830; 19, **Nebraska State Historical Society**, #M889-16; 20, ©G. Alan Nelson/**Dembinsky Photo Assoc.**; 21, **Nebraska State Historical Society**, #D4486; 22, **North Wind Picture Archives**; 25, ©SharkSong/M.Kazmers/**Dembinsky Photo Assoc.**; 26, ©**P. Michael Whye**; 27 (top), ©**Tom Tidball**; 27 (bottom), ©**P. Michael Whye**; 28 (top), ©**Cameramann International, Ltd.**; 28 (bottom), ©**Tom Dietrich**; 29, ©Dennis Mac Donald/**Unicorn Stock Photos**; 30-31, ©Donovan Reese/**Tony Stone Images, Inc.**; 32, ©James Blank/**Tony Stone Images, Inc.**; 33, ©James Blank/**Root Resources**; 34, ©**P. Michael Whye**; 35 (left), ©**Joan Dunlop**; 35 (right), MacDonald Photography/**Photri**; 36, ©**Tom Tidball**; 37, ©W.J. Scott/**H. Armstrong Roberts**; 38 (left), ©Jean Higgins/**Unicorn Stock Photos**; 38 (right), ©J. Urwiller/**H. Armstrong Roberts**; 39 (both pictures), ©**P. Michael Whye**; 40, ©**Tom Till**; 41 (top), ©Steve Vidler/**SuperStock**; 41 (bottom), ©Willard Clay/**Dembinsky Photo Assoc.**; 42, ©**Tom Dietrich**; 43, ©Tom Algire/**Tom Stack & Associates**; 44, **White House Historical Association**; Photograph by The National Geographic Society; 45, **Nebraska Historical Society**, #I392: 8-1; 46 (both pictures), **AP/Wide World Photos**; 47 (left), **Nebraska Historical Society**, # C363-2; 47 (right), **UPI/Bettmann**; 48, **AP/Wide World Photos**; 49 (both pictures), **AP/Wide World Photos**; 50 (top), **The Bettmann Archive**; 50 (bottom), **AP/Wide World Photos**; 51 (top), **AP/Wide World Photos**; 51 (bottom), **UPI/Bettmann**; 52, **AP/Wide World Photos**; 53, **AP/Wide World Photos**; 54 (top), **The National Arbor Day Foundation**; 54 (bottom), **Nebraska State Historical Society** #B649-137; 55 (top), **National Live Stock and Meat Board**; 55 (bottom), **Hebron Chamber of Commerce**; 56 (top), **Courtesy Flag Research Center, Winchester, Massachusetts 01890**; 56 (bottom), ©Rod Planck/**Dembinsky Photo Assoc.**; 57 (top), ©Tommy Dodson/**Unicorn Stock Photos**; 57 (middle), ©Rod Planck/**Tom Stack & Associates**; 57 (bottom), ©Skip Moody/**Dembinsky Photo Assoc.**; 58, ©**North Wind Pictures**, hand-colored engraving; 60-61, **Tom Dunnington**; back cover, ©**Tom Till**

INDEX

Page numbers in boldface type indicate illustrations.

63

ABOUT THE AUTHOR

Dennis Brindell Fradin is the author of 150 published children's books. His works for Childrens Press include the Young People's Stories of Our States series, the Disaster! series, and the Thirteen Colonies series. Dennis is married to Judith Bloom Fradin, who taught high-school and college English for many years. She is now Dennis's chief researcher. The Fradins are the parents of two sons, Anthony and Michael, and a daughter, Diana. Dennis graduated from Northwestern University in 1967 with a B.A. in creative writing, and has lived in Evanston, Illinois, since that year.